Spoke by Spoke Guidebook

Small Steps, Big Shifts for Navigating a WholeHearted Life

Terry Chase ND, MA, RN, CEIP-Ed

Spoke by Spoke Guidebook
Small Steps, Big Shifts for Navigating a WholeHearted Life

Copyright © 2025 by Terry Chase, ND, MA, RN, CEIP-ED
All rights reserved. No part of this book may be reproduced or copied
in any form without written permission from the publisher.

Push On Press, Grand Junction, Colorado
Contact the author: www.drterrychase.com

ISBN: 978-1-7378623-2-1

Some names and identifying details of individuals in this book
have been changed to protect their privacy.

Disclaimer

This experiential guidebook is intended for educational purposes only. The author does not provide medical or psychological advice, nor does this book serve as a substitute for professional care. The information and exercises within are designed to support self-reflection and opportunity for personal growth in the pursuit of a wholehearted life. Readers are encouraged to consult a licensed healthcare provider before implementing any practices that may have an impact on their physical, emotional, or mental well-being. The author assumes no responsibility for individual outcomes resulting from the use of this material.

Publishing assistance by BookCrafters, Parker, Colorado. www.bookcrafters.net
Editing assistance by Chris Nelson, Seattle, Washington.

Publisher's Cataloging-in-Publication Data

Names: Chase, Terry M., author.
Title: Spoke by spoke guidebook : small steps, big shifts for navigating a wholehearted life / Terry Chase, ND, MA, RN, CEIP-Ed.
Description: Grand Junction, CO: Push on Press, 2025.
Identifiers: ISBN: 978-1-7378623-2-1
Subjects: LCSH Self-actualization (Psychology) | Conduct of life. | Self-management (Psychology) | Self help. | BISAC SELF-HELP / Motivational & Inspirational | SELF-HELP / Personal Growth / General | SELF-HELP / Personal Growth / Self-Esteem | SELF-HELP / Self-Management / General | PSYCHOLOGY / Positive Psychology
Classification: LCC BF637.S4 .C43 2025 | DDC 646.7--dc23

Praise For.....
Spoke by Spoke Guidebook:
Small Steps, Big Shifts for Navigating a WholeHearted Life

You're not just holding a workbook - you have a life guide. Dr Terry Chase is a nationally-recognized speaker, author, teacher and coach who has risen through profound challenges to create a wholehearted life. Drawing on her deep experience and compassionate spirit, this workbook will help you reflect deeply, gain clarity, take action and navigate your way back to opening up fully to life.

~ **Melissa Ford, Business & Life Coach**

I can think of no better guide for navigating life-altering journeys than Dr. Terry Chase. This Guidebook will lead you through discovery of your own resources for post-traumatic growth, meaning-making and renewed purpose: devour Spoke by Spoke and thrive.

~ **Dr. Nancy Markham Bugbee, Psy.D, MA, MBA, BCC, COFOUNDER/ Clinical Director, Well-Being Center of Colorado (formerly Institute for Life & Care)**

Spoke by Spoke Guidebook is not just a companion for personal growth. The exercises helped me slow down, reconnect with myself, and uncover unexpected insights. Terry's gentle guidance and heartfelt wisdom make this book both practical and deeply moving. It's one I'll keep close—for myself and for my clients.

~ **Kamin Bell Samuel, PhD Transformational Business Coach and Filmmaker**

The Spoke by Spoke Guidebook: Small Steps, Big Shifts to Navigating a WholeHearted Life is the perfect companion to Terry's first book. Anyone seeking to live more intentionally will find value here—but it's especially powerful for those facing major life changes, whether joyful or painful. As I navigate divorce after 22 years and four kids, this book has given me something rare: hope. Even more, it offers meaningful prompts that help me find solid ground in a life that's been shaken. I'll be keeping it—and sharing it with others moving through big transitions.

~ **Wayne Herring, Growth Coach & Business Builder Camp Founder**

Sharing meaningful stories and thought-inducing exercises, Dr. Chase challenges readers to examine their own life journeys. Through reading her stories, introspection, and completion of the exercises, I am reminded that strength comes from within and that we can flourish despite life-altering challenges. This guidebook offers hope and inspiration to those facing life-altering health issues and points to the way to living fully.

~ **Pamela G. Coombs Delis PhD, RN**

Once again, Terry Chase has provided honesty and heart, turning pain into purpose and offers readers simple, powerful tools to do the same. Terry has a rare gift for transforming raw grief into clarity and resilience. Through her honest storytelling and accessible guidance, she invites readers to discover their own paths to healing and growth. Her journey is deeply personal—and yet universally relatable. The Guidebook helped me uncover what was missing in my life and gave me the strength to make meaningful change. A must-read for anyone ready to live more fully."

~ **Lynn Duncan, MSN, Associate Professor of Nursing and Clinical Education Center Coordinator, Colorado Mesa University**

Whether dealing with extraordinary factors and life crises or the expected, but unwelcome consequences of aging, this book provides inspiration to look beyond acceptance of limits and to motivate the reader to identify and enact changes that open doors to possibilities. The exercises serve as guidance in specific areas to help achieve goals the individual identifies. It is well worth reading.

~ **Susan Danner, MA, LPC, Cac III (Retired)**

Terry Chase has done it again! She uplifts and energizes, guiding us toward a life where even our wildest dreams, like riding horses or finding love in hard times, feel possible. This follow-up guidebook builds on Spoke by Spoke, offering practical insights from her powerful story of recovery after spinal cord injury. Her chapter on humor especially resonated with me. It's a reminder that joy can survive even our darkest days. If you or someone you know feels stuck, read these books. Terry Chase will help you know there's a way through.

~ **Sunny Roller, President, Post-Polio Health International Board of Directors**

Spoke by Spoke Guidebook is for anyone seeking guidance to move forward in their life toward what they hope for. Dr. Chase draws on her own journey of resilience to offer journal prompts and reflective actions to dig deep to find one's own resilience and inspiration. Whether you are at the beginning of a changing life season, or struggling through the trenches of life's challenges, this workbook can help to offer clarity and purpose.

~ **Dr. Veronica Lac, HERD Institute, Executive Director**

Spoke by Spoke Guidebook gives the reader a chance to look at their own challenges, guiding them to answer based on those challenges. Readers will find answers that work for their own personal growth and improvement.

~Susie Petrocco, Sr. Program Activities Director (ret) & Cancer Survivor

I was blown away by the perfect balance of self-compassion, resilience, and bad-assery Terry modeled for me in her memoir "Spoke by Spoke." This companion guidebook provides me with the opportunity to invite those same qualities into my own life. The workbook format allows for personalized engagement, making the experience unique to each reader. I love the combination of reflection and actionable steps toward making the changes identified as important to me. I especially appreciated the focus on humor and joy moving along this path to fuller lives.

~ **Pam Chiaro, Author, Cancer Survivor**

Terry's Spoke by Spoke Experiential Guidebook gave me opportunities to work through my own questions, issues, and struggles. Creative options such as art, writing, and physical activities can assist in exploration and healing. I really love this workbook!

~ **M. Peggy A. Rew, Wordsmith/Educator**

Dr. Terry Chase has created a powerful, user-friendly guidebook that multiplies the impact of her bestselling Spoke By Spoke! Highly recommended!!! It's a GREAT piece of work, Terry!

~ **Steve Chandler, Author of Time Warrior**

I love how this guidebook helps keep key ideas top of mind even after I've finished an exercise. Each Spoke of Insight continues to spark deeper reflection and days later, I'm still uncovering new perspectives on my thinking, priorities, and what I need to let go of. The book excerpts before each reflection are a standout feature. Dr. Chase writes with warmth and relatability, even as she shares experiences that are nearly unimaginable. The lessons learned and generously shared are truly inspiring. I've completed three Spokes of Insight so far and can't wait to dive into more.

~**Amy Archer, World Traveler**

Whatever it is that has broken your heart or your body, there is hope for healing right here in front of you. In her characteristically clear and compassionate voice, Dr. Terry Chase offers you not only her own deeply inspiring story of living after a paralyzing spinal cord injury, but also practical tools that can help you to create your own inspiring story of healing into an abundant, joyful whole-hearted life. This guidebook is a perfect follow-up to Spoke by Spoke, helping to bring those important messages into embodied, lived experience for the readers.

~ **Janet F. Quinn, PhD. Author,** *I Am a Woman Finding My Voice* **and Spiritual Director in private practice**

Acknowledgments

CREATING THIS *SPOKE BY SPOKE GUIDEBOOK* has been a journey shaped by many hands, hearts, and minds. I am deeply grateful to those who have supported, encouraged, and guided me along the way.

To the many participants in my WholeHearted Living coaching programs, personal growth retreats incorporating horses, and individual clients: you are the reason this work continues to grow. Your willingness to explore, reflect, and share insights has enriched the foundation of this guidebook.

To my editorial team, Jan and Joe McDaniel of BookCrafters and Chris Nelson whose dedication and attention to detail ensured that this guidebook remained true to its purpose while being clear, engaging, and accessible. Your thoughtful feedback and keen eyes have helped refine and shape these pages.

To my coaching mentors, colleagues, and friends: your encouragement, wisdom, and belief in this work have given me the strength to keep going.

To the many animals who have been my greatest teachers: my loyal dogs, whose steady companionship reminds me of the simple joys in life, and the horses, who continue to ground me in presence, connection, and trust.

To my family, whose love and support have been unwavering through all of life's twists and turns. Your presence in my life is a constant source of strength and inspiration. Especially to my loving partner, Sharon: thank you for being by my side, for laughter in the hard times, for adventure in the good times, and for always believing in me. I will love you forever.

And to Spirit, for the quiet whispers, deep wisdom, and constant guidance along the way.

This guidebook is a testament to the power of connection, learning, and transformation. May it serve as a companion and catalyst for all who embark on this WholeHearted Life journey.

With deep gratitude,
Dr. Terry Chase

Table of Contents

Welcome to this Experiential Guidebook..1
- Why This Experiential Guidebook?

Spoke 1: A Journey to WholeHearted Living..3
- One Step at a Time..5
    - A WholeHearted Life: One Step at a Time
- Building Resilience with Courage...9
    - Tough Call
- Embracing the Elements of Humor in Healing..13
    - Lighten Up

Spoke 2: Wisdom in Everyday Moments...17
- Finding Balance Amid Challenge...19
    - Is It a Crying Day or a Laughing Day?
- The Power of Simply Listening...22
    - She Listened
- Messages from a Mysterious Place...25
    - A Plain Whie Garment
- Take the First Step..28
    - Something Remarkable

Spoke 3: Shifting Perspective and Embracing Uncertainty.........................31
- Observing and Learning from Nature...33
    - Three White Bellies
- Shifting to a New Perspective...36
    - Looking Up
- Facing the Unknown..38
    - Backside of a Rock Face
- Listen at the Edge..41
    - Edge of Dark

Spoke 4: Moving Boldly into the Future 45
- Finding My Voice in Nursing 47
    - o Flinging Forward
- Very Hard Lessons 50
    - o Hard Lessons & Finding My Voice
- To See Myself First 53
    - o Be Bigger than My Chair
- The Power of Bearing Witness 56
    - o Welcome to America

Spoke 5: Connection, Healing & Growth 59
- Aliveness Is Real 61
    - o They Bring Me Alive
- Grounded in the Present Moment 64
    - o Breath & Body—Here & Now
- Learning While Doing 67
    - o Keep Riding, Keep Learning
- Learning and Growing Never End 70
    - o Keep Riding. Keep Learning.

Closing the Circle 73
- Transformation and Healing 75
    - o Windchime
- Embrace the Journey, Not the Destination 79
    - o A WholeHearted Life: It's Not About the Walking

Notes for My WholeHearted Journey 83
About the Author 93
Work with Dr. Terry Chase 94

To the many readers of...

*Spoke by Spoke: How a Broken Back
and a Broken Back Led to A WholeHearted Life* (2021).

Your inspiration has given me hope and promise
for the impact of living a WholeHearted Life!

I am grateful to you.

Welcome to this Experiential Guidebook

~

Why this Experiential Guidebook?

WELCOME TO *SPOKE BY SPOKE SMALL STEPS, BIG SHIFTS FOR NAVIGATING A WHOLEHEARTED LIFE*. This book is for you, the reader, to take time out for your own exploration to foster resilience, embrace balance, and live wholeheartedly.

In my first book, *Spoke by Spoke: How a Broken Back and a Broken Bike Led to a WholeHearted Life* (2021), I shared how experiencing a spinal cord injury challenged me, strengthened me and gave me the momentum to move forward. There were many readers who expressed appreciation for those stories, which inspired them in their own lives.

I developed this book as an opportunity for you to discover even more inspiration within yourself.

Perhaps you have not read *Spoke by Spoke*, or it's been a while since you have. What I've done in this book is select key chapters from *Spoke* and provide a short synopsis of each to give you the main ideas. Then, following the synopsis I've offered *Spokes of Insight* opportunities for you to reflect with a prompt, plus an activity or creative exercise to bring your ideas into action.

Maybe you're facing your own unexpected detour—a loss, a diagnosis, a change you didn't see coming. Maybe you're standing at a crossroads, unsure if you have the strength to take the next step. I know that feeling. I've lived it. And I also know that the next step—your step—is waiting.

This experiential guidebook is my offer, my way of paying forward the lessons I've learned. And now you can work through these processes for yourself. We all get stuck or lost at times, and we can choose to move forward, even when the road ahead looks nothing like what we imagined.

I encourage you to approach this guidebook with openness and curiosity. You can read it by itself, or you can read it alongside *Spoke by Spoke*. Set up a system that you can stick to, perhaps pacing yourself and setting out a weekly time to read a section, complete the reflection prompts and do the exercise.

Then notice how the writing reflections and actions steps stay with you through the following days or week. There are Notes for My Wholehearted Journey pages where you can make notes or revisit prompts and exercises over time to track growth.

The tools you might consider gathering are a writing utensil, colored pens, an extra notebook—in case you wish to write out more than the space in this book allows, or if you are reading this as an e-book.

This is a great time to practice kindness for yourself. Personal growth is not always easy, so make a quiet, comfortable space for yourself as you explore.

You may be wondering what a wholehearted life is and what that means for you. While I do not have a definite answer for you; I do know that creating a life that embraces positivity, stimulates a sense of purpose, connection with others and meaningful achievement are essential elements. I would encourage you to ask this question: what is your wholehearted life and what would you like to create moving forward. This guidebook will be useful in that pursuit.

Spoke 1

A Journey Toward Wholehearted Living

One Step at a Time

~

A Wholehearted Life

ONE MOMENT, I WAS FLYING DOWN A FAMILIAR ROAD, the Colorado wind in my face, strong and sure on my bike. The next, I was flying off my bike, the impact of an impaired driver's car stealing the ground from beneath me. Time split in half—the life I knew before and the one I would have to fight to build after.

I remember the heat of the car's hood, the weight of my body as it slammed onto the pavement. I was left behind, helpless on the road, my legs silent beneath me.

My bicycle, my trusted machine, was crumpled, soon tossed like evidence into the back of a police car as I was lifted into the back of an ambulance.

"Where are my legs?" I asked a stranger in brown boots, one of which I gripped tightly, holding onto the last bit of solidity I could find.

"Right here on the ground," he said, but I already knew. I couldn't feel them. I already understood that this was bad. And yet, in that moment, I had a choice: sink into panic or grasp onto whatever truth I could hold. As I clung to the man's boot, I chose presence.

In the ambulance, through waves of pain, I joked about the dull pea-green ceiling. If I could make a joke, I was still me. A new version, perhaps, but still me. The question was, who would I become now?

For a long time after that day, I wrestled with the reality of my new life. I was a thirty-two-year-old, strong, independent woman unwilling to be defined by a wheelchair. I fought the labels, the stereotypes, the well-meaning but misguided pity. I refused to let paralysis define me. And yet, what I learned over the years was that paralysis isn't just physical. It can reside in the stories we tell ourselves, the fear that keeps us from moving forward, the ways we convince ourselves we can't.

What I wanted—what I chose—was a wholehearted life. And that didn't mean just surviving. It meant living fully, taking risks, discovering what was still possible. It meant finding joy, pushing my limits, and redefining what strength looked like.

Step by step—spoke by spoke—I built a new life; one I never could have imagined back when I was gripping that stranger's boot. I kayaked in wild waters, handcycled up and over mountains, skied across landscapes I once thought I'd never touch again.

I found deep healing in the presence of horses, learned to trust my body in new ways, and invited love into my life. I learned that strength isn't just about physical muscles. It's about resilience, courage, and the willingness to adapt.

Spoke by Spoke Guidebook 7

Spokes of Insight

Reflection Prompt:
- Think about your "whole self."
- What are the major areas of your life?
- For example: personal growth, relationships, career, health, spiritual, recreation?

_____
_____
_____
_____
_____

Life Wheel Exercise:
- Divide the circle below into segments. Like a pizza!
- Label each segment with the areas of your life from the prompt.

- Reflect on how you are attending to each of those segments. Are any of these areas out of balance?
- Consider what area is out of balance and needs your attention.
- What next step will you take to bring that slice into balance?

_____
_____
_____
_____
_____

Building Resilience with Courage
~
Tough Call

THERE ARE MOMENTS WHEN LIFE SHIFTS IN AN INSTANT—when everything you've built is suddenly uncertain. For me, that moment came as I lay in a hospital bed, the phone pressed to my ear, speaking words that made my new reality undeniable.

"I can't make my summer assignments," I told the director of the Colorado Outward Bound School. "I've been in an accident. I'm in the hospital. My legs are partially paralyzed."

The very thing I had spent summers teaching: resilience, grit, pushing past limits—were now my own steepest mountain to climb.

The director's voice was full of care, but it was her last words that stuck with me. "Outward Bound will still be here when you're ready to return. There will always be a place for you in this school."

A place for me. Even in a wheelchair? Even in this body I barely recognized? That call could have been a closing door, but instead, I chose to hear it as a challenge.

For years, I had guided students through the wilderness, teaching them how to read mountainous terrain, set safety parameters, and move through the backcountry with confidence. Now, my survival depended on navigating a completely different landscape.

Instead of scouting trails, I was scanning sidewalks, parking lots, and doorways, constantly calculating whether a space was wide enough, smooth enough, safe enough. River crossings once required patience and planning—now, catching a bus or entering a restaurant took that same strategic thinking.

There were no maps for this kind of journey—not in the late 1980s.

So, I did what I had always done: I adapted. I read the landscape. I found a way.

Outward Bound teaches that nature doesn't make exceptions. If you don't stake your tent properly, the wind will take it. If you don't pack your bag well, the weight will punish you. I carried those lessons into this new life.

If I didn't take care of my spinal cord-injured body, there would be consequences:

serious ones. I had to relearn my body's signals, pay attention to temperature shifts, circulation, muscle strain. Things I once did without thinking now required precision. Like setting a secure anchor before rock climbing, my survival depended on thinking ahead, preparing for obstacles, and knowing when to rest.

I may not have been able to lead students across the mountains the way I once had, but the mountains still had lessons to teach me. Navigating life with a disability, finding solutions where others saw obstacles, holding onto purpose in the face of loss—this was its own kind of expedition.

In Outward Bound, I would always tell my students that the summit isn't the point—it's the journey that shapes you.

I kept going. Step by step. Always striving, never yielding.

Spokes of Insight

Reflection Prompt:
- Reflect on a time when you faced a major setback or challenge.
- What emotions did you feel in that moment?
- What actions helped you move forward, even if they were small steps?

_____
_____
_____
_____
_____

Resilience Roadmap Exercise:
- In the box below, see the metaphorical life roadmap with milestones marking challenges and lessons learned.
- Note major decisions, people, and experiences you encountered along the way.

Decision Matrix Exercise:

- Think about a current decision you are facing. Write it here now.
- Write in the two columns of the Decision Matrix below.
- What do I risk by saying yes?
- What do I risk by saying no?
- Reflect on these columns as you move forward in your decision-making process.

Risk by a YES	Risk by a NO
•	
•	
•	
•	
•	
•	
•	

Embracing the Elements of Humor in Healing

~

Lighten Up

I WAS SERIOUS. DEAD SERIOUS.

After the accident that shattered my body and stole my powerful legs, I buried myself in books—stories of resilience, survival, and miracles. I was searching for something, anything, that would tell me how to navigate this new reality. *Love, Medicine & Miracles: Lessons of Self-Healing (1988)* by Bernie Siegel, MD caught my attention. Dr. Siegel offered hope in the face of suffering, and I learned that people who processed their anger had better outcomes.

That concept stuck with me.

I wasn't dealing with my anger. I was stuffing it down, keeping it hidden under layers of grief, frustration, and forced composure. But emotions have a way of leaking out, and mine were seeping through the cracks.

Then came an unexpected visit that changed everything.

One evening, the intercom in my hospital room crackled to life.

"Terry, there's someone here to see you. Are you okay with her coming in for a short visit?"

"Terry, there's someone here to see you. Are you okay with her coming in for a short visit?"

"Who is it?" I asked, already annoyed.

The secretary responded, "*Sharon*," and a last name I did not recognize. I sighed. I was *busy* reading, thinking, *trying* to find answers. I didn't need a visitor, especially one whose name I didn't recognize. I sighed again and agreed to the visitor coming to my room.

I sighed. I was *busy* reading, thinking, *trying* to find answers. I didn't need a visitor, especially one whose name I didn't recognize.

"Who is it?" I asked, already annoyed.

The secretary responded, "*Sharon*," and a last name I did not recognize.

I sighed again and agreed to the visitor coming to my room.

Moments later, a woman walked in. She looked healthy, athletic, full of life—everything I felt I had lost. Sharon was a cyclist, I would later learn, fresh from completing the Ironman Triathlon in Hawaii.

"Hi, Terry," she said, all easy confidence. "I'm a friend of your friend Karen from Grand Junction. We know each other from softball. She asked if I'd stop by. How are you?"

How was I? I was lying in a hospital bed, my legs useless beneath me, tubes and machines surrounding me. But she didn't look at me with pity. She wasn't awkward or hesitant.

Before I could answer, she dropped another question:

"Did you know there's a talent show in the gym? How come you're not down there?"

Was she serious? A talent show? Featuring other patients? As if that was something I'd spend my time on?

"I'm reading," I responded flatly, holding up my book as proof of my serious pursuits.

She wasn't deterred. She made herself comfortable in the chair beside me, scanning the books stacked on my table.

"Oh, these are funny!" she said, picking up *Tales of the City* by Armistead Maupin. "Have you read these?"

I had not. I was too busy reading about life-and-death struggles, about healing and the mind-body connection.

But she started reading aloud. And laughing. And somehow—despite my irritation, my resistance, I found myself *loosening* just a little. Something about her presence chipped away at the armor I had wrapped around myself.

For the first time in what felt like forever, I let my guard down.

Before she left, Sharon looked at me with warmth and said, "Maybe you'll want to read these. They might help lighten you up a bit during this rehab thing."

She said it with such sincerity, such care, that it landed differently than anything else I had heard. No one had suggested that lightening up might actually *help*. That laughter might be necessary. That I didn't have to carry the weight of my injury so heavily.

Sharon had no idea that her visit would be a turning point for me. That this stranger who had walked into my room uninvited would become my life partner. That the woman who made me laugh when I wanted to remain angry would stay beside me for the next three decades.

She met me at my lowest, my most broken. And it didn't matter to her. She saw *me*.

She reminded me that I still had joy inside me. That I still had the capacity to laugh, to connect, to love.

And so, slowly, I began to lighten up.

Which, it turns out, was exactly what I needed for the long road ahead.

Spokes of Insight

Reflection Prompt:
- Recall a moment when humor helped you through a tough time. Write about how it shifted your perspective.
- Is there someone in your life who helps you lighten up? Who can bring a smile to your face and help you feel better just by their presence?
- Write a short thank you note to let them know.

_____
_____
_____
_____
_____

Humor Break Activity:
- Spend ten minutes finding humor in your day. Maybe it is a funny video featuring your favorite comedian, a humorous story, or an observation of something a little absurd.
- Journal about your reactions and how it makes you feel.
- And through the day, notice how that Humor Break affects your mood.

_____
_____
_____
_____
_____

Spoke 2

Wisdom
in Everyday Moments

Finding a Balance Amid Challenges
~
Is it a Crying Day or a Laughing Day?

EVERY MORNING, BEFORE I COULD EVEN PROCESS the weight of waking up in a hospital bed, the familiar voice of Earl the Pearl, my rehab tech, would cut through the thin curtain separating me from the rest of the world.

"Miss Terry, is this a crying day or a laughing day?"

It wasn't a joke. It wasn't small talk. It was a real question. And I never had the answer right away.

"I don't know, Earl," I'd say, still half-asleep. "I'll figure it out as we get going."

But let's be honest, most days in those early weeks were crying days.

The tears came without warning, without reason. They poured out as I lay there, feeling the absence of what had once been mine: strong, capable legs that had carried me up mountains, powered my bike down winding roads, and chased middle school kids across a soccer field. I grieved the loss of the body I had known, the freedom I had taken for granted, and even the simplest joys like running three miles with Shadow, my black lab beside me.

I was stuck in a place I never wanted to be. And the only way out was forward.

In those days, I found refuge in books, searching for insight from people who had lived through their own impossible circumstances. One thing became clear: suppressing grief, anger, and frustration would only hold me back. Learning from others, I had permission to feel all the sadness, the rage, the loss—but also to let it move through me. Holding it in would only trap me in a life I no longer recognized.

Earl understood this long before I did. She never judged. Never pushed me to "be positive" or "look on the bright side." She simply showed up, ready for whatever version of me she'd find that morning—whether I was tear-streaked or cracking a dry joke through the haze of frustration.

And if she could show up for me, I figured I had to show up for myself too.

My job was simple. Get out of bed. Get dressed. Get to meals. Go to therapy. Learn how to be in this new body. Learn how to navigate the world from this chair. It wasn't profound. It wasn't inspiring. It was just life—raw, unglamorous, relentless.

There was no magical epiphany, no moment when the heavens opened and granted me peace. The truth was, I had no choice but to move forward with what I had.

Earl let me take my time. She placed my clothes within reach, stood back, and let me struggle. It was painstaking at first, fumbling with socks, paralyzed and uncooperative feet, frustration mounting. But she never rushed me.

Some days, she'd chat as she tidied my room, sharing stories about her kids, her hardworking husband, their life together. Other days, she'd simply watch with knowing eyes, understanding the weight of what I was carrying without needing to say a word.

And then, one morning, something changed.

I was ready before she walked in. Clothes on, bed tidied, room in order. I had done it all myself.

She peeked in, expecting to start our usual routine, and her face broke into a proud, knowing grin.

"Well, look at you, Miss Terry!" I surprised her. But more importantly, I had surprised myself.

I used to think that healing would come when the crying stopped. That progress meant the laughter would take over, pushing out the grief. But I was wrong. Healing happened in the showing up.

Tears or laughter didn't matter. What mattered was that I didn't shut down. That I didn't let grief steal my energy. That I kept going, even when I wanted to disappear under the covers and pretend that none of this had happened.

Earl the Pearl, with her steady presence and quiet wisdom, had taught me life would go on again.

Laughing or crying either way.

Spokes of Insight

Reflection Prompt:
- Consider how you deal with emotions throughout the day.
- For example: stuff them down, deny them, let them rule you.
- Journal about how you balance emotional release in your life as positive or negative.
- What makes any day a "crying" or "laughing" day?

_____
_____
_____
_____
_____

Emotional Awareness Activity:
- At the start of each day this week, ask yourself: Is it a crying day, laughing day, or both?
- Put a SMILEY 😊 or CRYING ☹ Face on your calendar.
- Write a brief note about what makes it so.

_____
_____
_____
_____
_____

The Power of Simply Listening

~

She Listened

Some days, the weight of my new reality felt unbearable.

After hours of rehab—pushing, lifting, straining muscles that barely worked—I rolled into my hospital room, exhausted. Pressing the call button, I waited for help to get out of my clothes and stretch. The wheelchair felt heavier than ever.

Ten minutes passed. Then fifteen.

Finally, a young rehab tech walked in, slouched, uninterested. "You're lazy," he muttered.

I froze. What? Lazy? After hours of grueling therapy? After fighting for every movement?

"I'm really tired," I said tightly. "I just need a little help."

"Alright," he sighed. "What do you want me to do?"

Something in me snapped. My grip tightened on the wheel rims; my breath caught. "Never mind," I said abruptly. "I'm okay for now. Leave me alone."

He shrugged and walked out.

And so, I sat.

Through dinner. Through the evening. Through the sun sinking outside my window. Staring at the wall, motionless. His words had paralyzed me in a way my injury never had.

I hated this chair. I hated needing help. I hated everything about this.

A knock at the door broke the silence. Cathy, the evening nurse, stepped in. "Terry, I haven't seen you outside of your room tonight. What's going on?"

She pulled up a chair.

I hesitated. Then, quietly: "That rehab tech told me I was lazy." My voice cracked. "I am NOT lazy."

And just like that, the dam burst.

"I hate this. I hate being paralyzed. I work so hard, and I'm still weak. I don't like asking for help. And that guy—if he comes near me again, I'll spit at him!"

My chest heaved; my hands loosened their grip on my wheels.

Cathy listened. No rushing, no fixing. Just presence.

"Terry, I know for a fact you're not lazy. It's the last word I'd ever use to describe you." Her words landed softly but firmly.

"Let's get you out of those clothes and into bed," she continued. "I'll bring you a warm washcloth, some dinner, and your meds. Anything else?"

I exhaled, the weight in my chest was easing.

"No," I said, a small, tired smile appearing. "Thanks for listening."

Looking back, I realized Cathy was one of the people who inspired me to become a nurse. She didn't just do her job; she saw me. She knew when to sit in silence and simply listen.

And that made all the difference.

Spokes of Insight

Reflection Prompt:
- Recall a time when you experienced simply being listened to by another person. Write about what the experience was for you.
- How did that feel?
- What did you see?
- What did you notice about your emotions?
- How did your body react?

_____
_____
_____
_____
_____

Heart-Centered Listening Exercise:
- Take a moment to connect with your heart.
- One way to do that is to think of a special person, a special pet or something that connects you to those warm and loving feelings.
- Set an intention to practice simply listening to another person in a neutral, non-judgmental place.
- Reflect what you heard beneath the words.

_____
_____
_____
_____
_____

Messages from a Mysterious Place

~

A Plain, White Garment

SATURDAY AFTERNOON. I HAD JUST RETURNED from a rehab therapy outing to the mall, an exercise in re-learning how to navigate the world in a wheelchair. Maneuvering through racks of clothing, handling money at the food court, rolling across polished floors—it was all part of the test. I passed. But the weight of my new reality was still pressing down on me.

Back in my hospital room, I pressed the call button. Time to transfer to bed.

I waited. And waited.

A soft knock startled me. That's odd, I thought. Orderlies usually just burst in.

"Come in! I'm decent," I called.

A small, gray-haired woman stepped inside, moving carefully, almost reverently. I didn't recognize her. She wasn't part of my usual care team.

"I am…." she said a name I didn't recognize, one I'd forget almost instantly.

"Uh, hello," I replied, watching as she cradled a white garment in her arms.

"You have been blessed by this circumstance," she said gently. "There are great things ahead if you are willing to accept the blessings. I have brought you a garment, a symbol of this new life for you."

I sat there, uncertain. My Catholic upbringing had taught me to respect the mystical, but this was unlike anything I'd experienced before. I wasn't afraid—just still and silent, as if something beyond logic was unfolding.

She extended the garment toward me. It was simple, white, embroidered at the neckline, with no store tags or labels. Handmade.

"Okay, thank you" I said at last, curiosity outweighing skepticism. I took the garment and laid it across my lap.

Then, as quietly as she had entered, she turned and walked out.

The door swung open again almost immediately.

"Okay! Ready for that transfer?" The orderly bustled in, oblivious to the woman who had just left.

"Did you see that lady?" I asked.

"Nope," he replied casually. "Didn't see anyone."

Without another word, he helped me into bed, removed my shoes, and pulled a sheet over me. The white garment was hung in the closet without a second glance.

For years, I told no one about the woman or the garment—not the nurses, not my doctors, not even Earl the Pearl. Yet, decades later, I still have that garment.

Was she an angel? A kind stranger? A figment of my exhausted imagination? I don't know.

But I do know this: My spinal cord injury became a gateway to blessings I never could have imagined. That simple garment, and the message it carried, became a quiet promise I made to myself—to accept both the challenge and the gift of this new life.

And I have.

Spokes of Insight

Reflection Prompt:
- Consider what you think of as mysteriousness in your life: being alive, the place of your birth and family situation.
- It could be like in this story, or even something more subtle, such as a strange coincidence.
- What was that like for you? Did you dismiss it or take the message into your life?
- As you remember it, what was the message you took away from the experience?
- Is there an action step related to the experience or message that you might take forward into your life now?

_____
_____
_____
_____
_____

Creative Art Exercise:
- Gather some blank paper, old magazines, stickers and coloring pens.
- Make a collage of words, pictures, and symbols that reflect this mysterious experience and what message you received.

Take the First Step

~

Something Remarkable

Fifty days into rehab, and I was nearly ready to leave.

I could transfer myself in and out of bed, dress, shower, and move independently in my wheelchair. The metal brace holding my spine upright would come off soon. But what truly saved my sanity during those long weeks wasn't just regaining daily function, it was movement, the chance to feel like an athlete again.

That's why Tuesday was a big deal—I was cleared to go waterskiing on this special therapeutic recreation outing.

I barely slept the night before. At dawn, I was up and ready. Nurses ensured my medications were swallowed, personal care completed and a hot cup of coffee ready.

By 6:00 a.m., I was on the specially equipped bus heading to Boulder Reservoir.

The lake was glass—calm, empty, all ours. No other boats allowed. Just me, the adaptive sports program staff, ski boats, disabled skiers and the open water.

I rolled down the dock toward a customized sit-ski—a plastic chair bolted onto two wide skis, with a tow rope fixed to the back of the boat. My feet were strapped in, body secured. Then came the shock—the frigid morning lake swallowing me as they lowered me into the water.

I turned toward the boat, took a deep breath, and yelled:

"Hit it!"

The boat surged forward, and suddenly the ski lifted, cutting through the water as spray hit my face. I held on tight, the world whipped by. I was waterskiing.

Two full laps around the reservoir, wind in my hair, face aching from smiling. The cold vanished, replaced by sheer exhilaration.

That morning became my claim to fame—waterskiing before I was even discharged from rehab.

And I didn't stop there.

After my discharge and return to real life, I went back. My skills sharpened. I transitioned to a lighter adaptive ski, started holding my own rope, and eventually mastered the perfect landing, skiing in without a spill, my hair still dry.

But waterskiing wasn't just waterskiing.

It was control in a world that felt unpredictable. It was testing my limits, finding strength in struggle, proving to myself that I could adapt, could push through fear, could embrace this new life.

Some days, I took my frustrations out on that lake—slapping the water, carving into turns, releasing the anger of living in a body that no longer did what I wanted it to. And every time, the water held me.

If I could handle the unpredictable waters of Boulder Reservoir, I could handle just about anything.

And so far, that's turned out to be true.

Spokes of Insight

Reflection Prompt:
- What's Something Remarkable?
- Spend at least ten minutes to remember Something Remarkable in your life.
- Write about that memory and details of what made it remarkable to you.

_____
_____
_____
_____
_____

Something Remarkable Exercise:
- What small victories or moments of joy have you experienced this week? How did they contribute to your overall well-being?
- Make a collage of Something Remarkable you want to do.
    - o   Make a collage of words, pictures, symbols that reflect Something Remarkable.
- What would you have to let go of to take that Remarkable step?

Spoke 3

Shifting Perspective and Embracing Uncertainty

Observing and Learning from Nature
~
Three White Bellies

Eight brightly colored sea kayaks bobbed in the Pacific off the coast of Washington's San Juan Islands. The small group of paddlers were lined up, side by side, waiting. This was orca day—the highlight of our three-day paddle trip, the reason we had come.

Tim, our burly trip leader, grinned. "Sixteen years out here, and the orcas never disappoint. I just don't know exactly when or where they'll show up."

We sat in silence, tucked against a granite rock wall, floating amidst seaweed and kelp. Then, a shout from the paddler in the red kayak:

"Look! There they are!"

Three hundred yards away, black fins pierced the water's surface, sleek bodies gliding north in tight pods. They rose and fell, breath geysers misting in the sun. My breath quickened. Cameras clicked, capturing the massive, glistening giants as they followed their ancient migratory path.

For a moment, I forgot my wheelchair. I was simply here, bobbing on the edge of the ocean, watching something primal and powerful unfold before me.

Then, something changed.

At the far end of the lineup, I noticed three whales breaking away. Unlike the others, they weren't continuing north. They were coming toward us.

At first, I kept snapping pictures, but then—*Oh, shit*. They weren't slowing down.

"Look left!" I yelled. "Orcas are coming right at us!"

Heads turned just as the three whales, massive and undeniable, closed the distance. The water beneath us swelled, surging with their unseen power. And just before reaching our fragile plastic boats, they did something unexpected—

They rolled, belly up.

Three white bellies flashed beneath the surface, then *whoosh*! They shot underneath us, their force lifting our kayaks in a single, giant swell. I felt it—a connection of muscle, motion, and pure energy. If they had flicked their tails or breached at the wrong moment, we'd have been tossed like driftwood.

But they didn't.

And then, just as quickly as they'd come, they were gone, rejoining the pod, disappearing into the expanse of the sea.

Not a single kayak overturned. No one was hurt. It was over in seconds.

That night, scrolling through my camera, I saw it: the three enormous black fins slicing toward me, the white underside flipping just before impact. And suddenly the weight of what had happened settled in.

Why us? What made them break formation, divert from their well-worn highway, and slip so deliberately beneath our boats?

For days, weeks, years, I carried the question. They could have crushed us with a flick of a tail, shattered our kayaks with their sheer size. But instead, they touched us—deliberately, gracefully.

I wasn't just watching the whales that day.

I was with them.

And for that moment, floating in the wake of their passing, I was something more than just a person in a kayak. I was part of something ancient, something vast, something wild.

Spokes of Insight

Reflection Prompt:
- Go outside if you can or gaze from a window. Spend ten minutes observing the elements of nature.
- Journal about what you notice in this observation.
- Note how this connects to you and your personal growth.

_____
_____
_____
_____
_____

Creative Arts Activity:
- I shared in the story about the whales how it was for me to see them coming toward the group of kayaks.
- Now, imagine three white bellies coming toward you. What do they symbolize and what messages do they bring?
- Draw the images and write about the messages they bring to you.
- As you listen to the messages, what is one step forward you will take in response to them?

_____
_____
_____
_____
_____

Shifting to a New Perspective
~
Looking Up

THERE'S SOMETHING ABOUT A CRISP FALL DAY that makes me feel alive—the bite of cool air, the rustle of golden leaves, the promise of movement. That day on the field, it wasn't just my middle school students who were learning the flag football game. I was, too.

Just five months earlier, my life had changed in an instant. A crash. A broken back. A body that no longer worked the way I had always known. But there I was—whistle in hand, calling plays, making sure every kid was in the game. No one sat on the sidelines in my PE class. Including me.

Standing upright with the help of my crutches, I felt the old fire return. The game was in motion, kids were laughing, running, reaching—until suddenly, the world tilted. One moment I was coaching, the next, I was flat on my back, staring up at a circle of wide-eyed seventh graders. The cheering had stopped.

"Miss Chase, are you okay?" The concern in their voices was real.

A body scan. No pain. A deep breath. Still breathing. A check-in with my heart—yep, still wildly in love with these kids and this work. And then, laughter.

"Yes! I'm fine!" I grinned from the grass. "And I am so happy to be here, back in the game with you all!"

I wanted these kids to know life knocks us down. Sometimes hard. Sometimes in ways we never see coming. But there's always a way back up. Always.

So, I did what I had learned to do. I adapted. I turned over, pulled myself to my wheelchair, and got back in the seat that was now part of my life. The kids were still watching, still holding their breath. I brushed the grass from my hair, grinned, and shouted, "Alright, game's not over! Let's play!"

The lesson wasn't about football that day. It was about resilience. About showing up, even when life doesn't go as planned. About knowing that falling isn't the end—it's just another view. A moment to look up, to see the faces around me to remember why I'm here.

And then? I got back in the game.

Spokes of Insight

Reflection Prompt:
- Write about a time in your life when you had to "look up" to change your perspective.
- What did you do?

_____
_____
_____
_____
_____

Looking Up Exercise:
- Go to an outdoor space, perhaps your own backyard or a local park. Find a comfortable surface to lie on your back and spend ten minutes looking at the sky.
- Notice how this changes your perspective.
- Write down a few words or phrases that arise from this new perspective.

_____
_____
_____
_____
_____

Facing the Unknown
~
Backside of a Rock Face

I SAT IN MY WHEELCHAIR AT THE BASE OF THE ROCK WALL, once again looking up. The students, their faces a mix of excitement and nerves, were gearing up for the day's rappel. I had done this before—many times, in fact. As an Outward Bound instructor, I had led teenagers through the wilderness, teaching them how to push past fear, how to trust themselves. But that was before. Before my body changed. Before my world changed.

Now, I was supposed to sit this one out, watching from below.

Then came Tom's voice—loud, sure, and full of possibility. "Let's get you up there, Terry! You can do the rappel—show the kids how it's done!"

I laughed. Sure. How?

Tom had an answer: a horse.

Joe was a tall, white horse and he walked toward me, with his head high, his eyes steady. The sight of him sent a wave of emotion through me, an old memory surfacing of the first horse I had cared for as a teenager. Could I do this? Could I climb onto his back, trust him to carry me where my legs could not?

Fear whispered no. But something deeper, something stronger, whispered yes.

With the help of my team, I was lifted onto Joe's back, my arms wrapped tight around Tom's waist. No saddle. No stirrups. Just trust. As Joe moved up the narrow, winding trail, I felt a rush of something I hadn't felt in a long time—freedom. The same wind that had once brushed against my face as I hiked these mountains now carried me forward on the back of a horse.

At the top, I slid off Joe and landed on the soft earth. No wheelchair. Just me, sitting on the mountainside, exactly where I belonged.

My students were waiting, their faces full of awe—not because of what I couldn't do, but because of just what I had done. I saw in them a truth I had always taught: courage isn't about eliminating fear—it's about stepping across the edge despite it.

I strapped on the harness, checked the ropes, and scooted to the edge of the rock face. One deep breath. One final push off. And just like that, I was rappelling down, gravity pulling me into the unknown.

The lesson of the day was clear—not just for my students, but for me. Life will always bring us to edges we never expected. The question is: Do we let fear keep us there? Or do we trust, lean in, and take the leap?

That day, with the help of Joe, Tom, and the students who looked up to me, I flung myself forward once again.

Spokes of Insight

Reflection Prompt:
- Reflect on a time when trust (in yourself, in a person, or in a process) helped you move through uncertainty.
- What emotions surfaced? How did you respond?
- In hindsight, what helped you step forward despite fear? How did it shape your experience?

_____

_____

_____

_____

_____

Take a Leap Exercise:
- Identify an area in your life where you feel "stuck" or hesitant to move forward.
- As you consider one courageous step, think about how FEAR and TRUST influence your decisions.
- Make notes in the two columns "FEAR Says" and "TRUST Says". For example:
    - FEAR Says: write about the doubts, worries, and beliefs that limit you from taking action and staying stuck.
    - TRUST Says: write about the strengths, possibilities and supports that encourage you to act and move forward.

Fear Says	Trust Says
•	
•	
•	
•	
•	
•	

Listening At the Edge

~

Edge of Dark

THE DESERT STRETCHED BEFORE ME, raw and endless, the Green River cutting through the canyon below like an old scar. Sitting in my wheelchair at the edge, the wind swirling sand around my tires, staring into the abyss. It wasn't just a view—it was an invitation.

The thought flickered through my mind: *What if I just rolled forward? What if I let go?*

I wasn't planning to die. Not exactly. I just wanted out of the metal frame that confined me, out of the relentless reality of a life that had changed without my permission. Before the accident, I would've been on my bike, pedaling hard alongside my friend Al, feeling the burn in my legs, my breath in sync with the wild rhythm of the trail.

Now, I was here waiting, watching, remembering what it felt like to move freely.

The darkness had been whispering to me for months. It found me in the everyday moments: in the sideways glances from strangers, the forced smiles, the empty parking spaces marked with a symbol that now defined me. It followed me into the doctor's office, where a young physician barely looked up as he evaluated my "level of function." It screamed at me in the sterile, clinical language of disability assessments, reducing my existence to a checklist of limitations.

And sometimes, the dark didn't whisper at all.

It screamed.

The weight of it all—the grief, the anger, the relentless exhaustion of proving my worth—settled like a boulder on my chest.

But something always pulled me back.

Maybe it was the students who looked up to me, as a teacher, needing me to show up.

Maybe it was the therapist who held space for my rage and grief.

Maybe it was the stubborn, unrelenting part of me that refused to let the darkness win.

Slowly, painfully, I realized that running from the darkness wasn't the answer. I had to step into it, feel every ounce of pain, and then find my own way through.

So, I did.

I learned to *move* again—not in the same way, but in ways I never imagined. I took up hand cycling, propelling myself forward with the strength in my arms. I paddled into the wilderness in a sea kayak, felt the cool rush of water against my hands. I skied, I swam, I rode horses. I reclaimed movement, reclaimed myself.

And in the process, I discovered something unexpected: *I was more alive than I had ever been.*

The edge of the dark will always be there. It waits for all of us in different ways. But I learned that I don't have to go to that edge of dark and fall in.

I can stand—no, *I can rise*.

And so can you.

Spokes of Insight

Reflection Prompt:
- Imagine standing at the edge of a dark forest, a deep canyon or a wide body of water. Write about how you feel and what might lie beyond those dark edges of uncertainty.
- How might you rewrite the story with a focus on lessons learned and that moment shaped you for the better?

_____
_____
_____
_____

Step with Courage Activity:
- As you have done in previous chapters, consider one courageous step toward something that feels uncertain. What is one small step for you to take?
- Now with courage take that one small step forward. Think about what one small step is for you.
- Reflect on how you did and how you felt having taken that one small step.

_____
_____
_____
_____

Spoke 4

Moving Boldly into the Future

Finding My Voice in Nursing
~
Flinging Forward

HOW DOES A WOMAN IN A WHEELCHAIR BECOME A NURSE? How does she endure four years of grueling coursework, 4,000 hours of clinical training, and prove—again and again—that she belongs? The short answer: she flings herself forward.

When I first read about the Nursing Doctorate Program at the University of Colorado, I didn't stop to wonder if my wheelchair would be a barrier. The program called to me as a blend of science, the arts, and human caring that resonated with my experience as both a patient and a teacher. I applied with conviction, confident in my credentials, only to receive a swift rejection.

This hit harder than expected. Was it my injury? My wheelchair? Had they assumed, without ever speaking to me, that I couldn't handle the physical demands? The sting of that rejection made one thing clear—I *had* to reapply.

I scheduled a meeting with the program director, a woman whose office walls were lined with degrees and honors. When I asked why I was denied, she said.,"The committee had concerns about whether you could perform CPR."

Cardiopulmonary Resuscitation is the ability to get on the floor and save a life. I had been dismissed based on an assumption that being in a wheelchair would prevent that life-saving action.

"I *can* do CPR," I told her. "I've practiced it, been certified in it. I know how to get to the ground safely and do what needs to be done. I'm not asking for special treatment—I am asking for the chance to prove I can be a nurse."

That moment was like so many in my post-accident life—having to fight to be seen as capable, to push back against doubt. I explained why I wanted to be a nurse: not for the title, but because I had *been* the patient, and I knew firsthand the difference a truly caring nurse could make. I wasn't here to prove anything to myself—I was here because I had something to give.

I rewrote my application. I refined my arguments. And this time, I was accepted.

The next four years tested me in ways I hadn't imagined, including practical ones. The nursing school building, for example, was minimally retrofitted for only *sort of* worked for someone in a wheelchair. I had to navigate both physical and systemic obstacles, proving again and again that I could do the job.

But what I learned in that program went beyond the nursing knowledge and the clinical training. I learned that resilience isn't about being fearless. It's about moving forward *despite* fear. It's about adapting, problem-solving, and knowing, deep down, that you belong—even when others aren't sure you do.

I started that program as the only wheelchair user in my cohort. I finished as a nurse, ready to serve.

Because when life dares you to sit still, the only choice is to fling yourself forward.

Spokes of Insight

Reflection Prompt:
- Reflect on the story of Flinging Forward. What comes to mind?
- What would "flinging forward" in your life look like?
- List three small steps to move forward.
- What would be important as you consider this process?

_____
_____
_____
_____
_____

Creative Arts Activity:
- Gather some blank paper, old magazines, stickers and coloring pens.
- Make a collage of words, pictures and symbols that reflect you flinging forward into your future.
- Have fun and give yourself permission to go for it!
- Write a few thoughts about your Creative Arts Activity:

_____
_____
_____
_____
_____

Very Hard Lessons

~

Hard Lessons

I ENTERED NURSING SCHOOL WITH A CLEAR VISION of what it meant to be a nurse—building trust, breaking down barriers, and helping patients heal. What I hadn't expected was starting with bed-making, bed baths, and bedpans. These tasks felt tedious, even beneath me. I wanted to get to the *real* work of nursing—the deep, human connection that had drawn me to this field.

One day, my frustration boiled over and said to my instructor, "I thought this was about human caring, not just cleaning bedpans."

Kind but firmly, she set me straight, "Ms. Chase, if we can't meet a patient's basic physical needs, they won't be ready for anything else."

That lesson hit hard. I had been thinking of nursing in lofty idealistic terms, but it was also hands-on, down-and-dirty. Whether making a bed, washing a mannequin's face, or handling a bedpan, I began to see that *this* was human caring.

As I threw myself into my clinical work, another realization surfaced—I was in denial about my own time as a patient. Learning to care for others forced me to face what I had once endured. I thought I was preparing to serve others, but I was also confronting my own past.

Finding My Voice

"Pair up," Professor Janson announced. "One person will be the patient, the other will practice range-of-motion exercises."

I knew this routine well—therapists had stretched and moved my legs every day in rehab. Now, it was my turn to do it for someone else. But unlike my classmates, I was in a wheelchair, and my partner, Jeff, was lying in a hospital bed.

"Alright," I said. "Jeff, I'll need your help."

He grinned. "Oh, right. I forgot you were in a wheelchair."

I took that as a compliment.

We lowered the bed so I could reach him, and I stretched his leg, feeling the strain in my arms. Just as I found my rhythm, Professor Janson appeared.

"Miss Chase, show me that again."

I did. Again. And again. With every repetition came another correction. More scrutiny. More feedback than I had ever seen her give another student. By the end of class, I was sweating—and seething.

I waited until the others left and asked to speak with her.

"I feel like I'm under a microscope," I said, keeping my voice steady. "It's like you're waiting for me to fail."

She sighed. "Terry, I'm worried about your safety. In my twenty-five years as a nurse and professor, I've never seen a nurse in a wheelchair."

There it was. The unspoken doubt finally spoken aloud.

"Professor," I said, "nurses are problem-solvers. I'm adapting, just like any good nurse. I will always ask for help when I need it, but I *can* do this."

She studied me, then nodded. "I trust you'll speak up if you need help."

"I will," I said.

The scrutiny eased, but I knew this was just the beginning. The barriers weren't only physical. They were in people's minds. And sometimes, in my own mind.

Spokes of Insight

Reflection Prompt:
- Think about a time when you resisted learning something because it felt too basic or beneath you.
- How did that resistance shape your experience?
- Looking back, what did you ultimately learn from that experience?
- How does this apply to your life now?

_____
_____
_____
_____
_____

Reframe the Basics Exercise:
- Identify one daily task or responsibility that feels tedious or frustrating.
- For one week, note your observations each day.
- Ask yourself: How does this contribute to my growth? How does this connect me to others? Approach this task with the mindset that it is foundational to something bigger.
- How did your mindset affect your experience? Did new insights emerge? How might this practice help you navigate future challenges?

_____
_____
_____
_____
_____

To See Myself First

~

Be Bigger Than My Chair

Nursing school wasn't just about textbooks, clinical rotations, or grueling late-night study sessions in the university library. It was about something deeper, something I had to learn for myself over four long, demanding years: I had to be bigger than my chair.

Every time I rolled into a new hospital unit, a community clinic, or even a locked adolescent psych ward, I had a choice—let others see *only* the wheelchair, or make sure they saw *me first*. I chose the latter. It wasn't easy. It took energy I didn't always have. It meant proving myself over and over again, not just as a nursing student but as a competent, confident professional who belonged in this space. There were moments when I questioned if it was worth it—when exhaustion set in, when self-doubt crept in, when I thought icing donuts at a bakery might be a whole lot easier than pushing myself up that steep, concrete ramp outside the Nursing School.

And yet, I stayed.

Through rotations in mother-baby units, migrant community health, the ER, and even geriatrics, I built a foundation of clinical expertise. I honed my skills, developed instincts, and tested my endurance—not just physically but emotionally. And in a full circle moment, I found myself back at the very hospital in Grand Junction where, just five years earlier, I had been the patient, fighting for my own survival.

But here's the truth: the toughest battles weren't just about proving myself to others. They were about proving myself to me.

I had spent years feeling like I was under the spotlight, convinced everyone was scrutinizing my every move, waiting for me to stumble. But somewhere along the way, I realized that the most intense scrutiny wasn't coming from my professors, preceptors, or peers—it was coming from within.

I was the one holding myself to impossible standards. I was the one turning up the heat.

The moment I crossed that graduation stage—one of thirteen students earning a Nursing Doctorate, I knew I was transformed. Not because I had checked off the requirements, not because I had "proven" my place, but because I had answered the call that had been pulling at me since the beginning.

I was no longer a student trying to become something.

I *was* a nurse.

A nurse in a wheelchair.

A nurse ready to push past expectations—my own and everyone else's.

What I didn't know then was that this was only the beginning.

Spokes of Insight

Reflection Prompt:
- Think about a time when you felt you had to prove yourself to others.
- What were you trying to prove? Who (or what) did you feel was holding you back?
- Now, looking at that situation with fresh eyes, what was the biggest challenge external or internal?
- Journal your insights and reflect: Where in your life do you need to be bigger than your chair?

_____
_____
_____
_____
_____

See Yourself First Exercise:
- Identify one situation in your life where you feel like others might see a limitation before they see *you*. For example: a job role, a personal challenge, or even a self-imposed belief.
- Write down three ways you can shift presenting yourself in that space and make sure your *presence* is seen first. For example: adjusting body language, using direct eye contact and a strong handshake, maybe even changing your internal self-talk before entering the room.
- Over the next week, practice stepping into that space with intention.
- Each time, check in: How did you feel? How did others respond? What changed when *you* led with confidence?

_____
_____
_____
_____
_____

The Power of Bearing Witness
~
Welcome to America

BY THE TIME I REACHED MY NEUROTRAUMA EXTERNSHIP at a major Denver medical center, I had learned how to handle complex cases. I was confident in my skills, my ability to advocate for patients, and my presence in the room as a nurse, not just a student, and certainly not just a woman in a wheelchair. But nothing could have prepared me for Bin.

Bin was twenty-four years old, a young man who had risked everything to come to America in search of freedom. Instead, he found himself trapped in a detention center, hopeless and alone. His attempt to end his life didn't result in him taking his last breath, but it did take everything else—his awareness, his movement, his future. By the time I met him, his body was functioning, but his mind was lost in the unreachable distance of a vegetative state. He had no voice.

And yet, I knew there was still something we could give him.

In a tense meeting with his care team, I made a request: If we got his family on the phone, I wanted them to have the chance to speak to him, even if he couldn't respond. I knew, deep in my bones, what it meant to be spoken *to* rather than spoken *about*. I had once been patient trapped in a broken body, completely dependent on others for survival. I had fought to reclaim my voice. But Bin had no such opportunity. His parents, still in rural China, needed the chance to say goodbye. And he needed to *hear* them, on whatever level was possible.

At first, the room hesitated. He was unresponsive. Comatose. What was the point? But I didn't back down.

Finally, Dr. Joseph nodded. "Let's arrange the call."

Days later, I sat beside Bin as the phone call finally connected. I held the receiver to his ear as his parents, speaking from halfway across the world, poured out their love, their sorrow, their final words to the son they would never see again. Though he couldn't answer, I knew that on some level, he could still receive.

His parents made the heartbreaking decision to withdraw life support. In the days that followed, we kept him comfortable as his body slowly let go. He passed in the middle of the night, peacefully.

But my care for him didn't end there.

When I asked what would happen to his ashes, the response was indifferent—they would likely remain unclaimed. That wasn't good enough. I got permission to take them myself.

Weeks later, I drove with Sharon to the top of Jones Pass, high above the tree line where the sky is endless, and the air is crisp. Sitting in my wheelchair on the rocky mountaintop, I opened the bag of ashes, held them up to the wind, and whispered a final farewell.

Then, as they scattered into the vast American sky, I shouted into the wind:

"Welcome to America!"

Spokes of Insight

Reflection Prompt:
- Consider a time when you had the opportunity to speak up for someone who could not advocate for themselves.
- Did you take that opportunity? If so, what happened? If not, what held you back?
- How could your voice and your presence have changed at that moment?
- Reflect and Write: What does it mean to honor someone's life, their voice, or their presence, even when they can't speak for themselves?

_____
_____
_____
_____

The Power of Bearing Witness Activity:
- Identify someone in your life—past or present—who may feel unheard, unseen, or powerless. For example: a friend, a family member, a colleague, or even someone in your community.
- Take one intentional action to acknowledge their presence and affirm their dignity. For example, this could be listening without distraction, asking about their story, advocating for their needs, or simply offering kindness in a moment that might otherwise go unnoticed.
- Journal your experience. What did you observe? How did the other person respond? How did it feel to bear witness to their humanity?

_____
_____
_____
_____

Spoke 5

Connection, Healing and Growth

Aliveness Is Real

~

They Bring Me Alive

I RODE WELL TODAY. NOT PERFECTLY, BUT WELL. Sitting deep in the saddle, trusting the rhythm of the horse beneath me, feeling the subtle communication between us—the shift of weight, the flick of an ear, the steady rise and fall of breath. Thirty minutes around the dusty indoor arena, muscles engaged, mind focused, body both strong and vulnerable. "Head in the middle and a leg on each side," an old cowboy once told me. Simple wisdom, but for me, a profound truth.

I wasn't always at home in the saddle after the accident. The injury took my legs, stole my ability to run, to climb, to race up mountains like the tomboy I once was. But horses—they gave me something back. They shook loose the stuck parts of me, the grief I didn't even know I carried, and pieced me back together in a way that felt more whole. More honest. More *alive*.

In the coming pages, you'll meet the horses who became my teachers. They weren't blank slates or mindless machines. They had histories—some were champions in the show ring, some worked cattle, others spent their years chasing down steers in a rodeo arena. And in their old age, they stepped into a new role: guiding me back to myself.

Horses demand presence. They don't care about your past or your story—only how you show up *right now*. They require honesty, not just in your movements, but in your heart. When I ride, there is no pretending, no mask, no posturing. Just the truth of the moment: am I here, fully, with them? Or am I lost in old fears, old wounds?

They have taught me patience. Strength. How to listen, how to trust. How to let go.

And maybe, in their stories, you'll find something for yourself too. Isn't that what we all need? A way back to ourselves. A way to feel fully alive again.

Spokes of Insight

Reflection Prompt:
- I have learned that horses respond to what humans bring in the moment. For example: emotions, energy, awareness.
- Think of a time when you were with an animal—horse or otherwise—and felt truly seen.
- How did they respond to you?
- How did that interaction shift your awareness or emotions?

_____

_____

_____

_____

- In my story, I mention how the horse shook up my "stuck parts" and brought a sense of wholeness.
- Have you ever had an experience—whether with an animal, in nature, or through movement—that made you feel more alive? Describe the moment and what it awakened in you.

_____

_____

_____

_____

Presence: Experiential Activity

- Spend 10–15 minutes in the presence of an animal (a horse, a dog, a bird, even watching wildlife from a window).
- As you observe without judgement or analysis, what do you notice in the animal's body language? How do they respond to your presence?
- Write freely about what you observed and felt. What emotions rise within you? Did you notice any resistance, fear, or moments of connection?
- What lessons surfaced about trust, presence, or self-awareness?

_____

_____

_____

_____

_____

Grounded in the Present Moment

~

Breath and Body—Here and Now

It started as another step forward—another training program, another challenge. This time with horses.

I had already spent years training to be a Gestalt therapist, learning the power of presence, of truly being in the moment. But this program, Gestalt-Equine Psychotherapy, brought something new. Horses—masters of non-verbal communication, creatures who live entirely in the now. No pretense, no masks, no past regrets or future anxieties, just the raw, undeniable truth of the moment.

I was drawn in. Not just by the psychology of it, but by the promise of connection, of learning from a partner who had no judgment, only presence.

It didn't matter that I used a wheelchair. I wanted this. *All of it.*

But wanting something and being ready for it are two different things.

On one of our intensive training weekends, Duey asked, "Terry, you ready to jump in?"

I wasn't sure. Not really. But I said yes. I always said yes.

William, a fellow student, would be my assigned therapist for the session. We met at the arena gate. "Let's start with your body," he said. "Take a breath. Notice what's there."

I pushed my wheelchair through the deep sand, making my breath ragged. And I *felt that old frustration rising again.* The struggle. The exhaustion of always having to push harder, to keep up, to prove that I *belonged* in spaces like this.

The horse, a bay mare with seemingly wise eyes, stood still as I approached. Horses didn't care that I was in a wheelchair. They saw energy, not limitations. They responded to truth, not pretense. And right now, I wasn't being honest—not with myself, not with the horse.

William handed me the lead rope. "Just notice," he said.

I did. And then, the horse pulled away.

I tightened my grip. She pulled harder.

"What's happening?" William asked.

"I don't know," I snapped. "She's leaving. She's not paying attention to me."

And then, the dam broke.

"I'm tired," I blurted out. "I'm tired of struggling. I'm tired of feeling like I have to keep up. I'm *angry*—at this wheelchair, at my body, at how damn hard everything is!"

My hands loosened on the rope. My shoulders slumped. And then—*the horse turned back to me.*

She stood close, her head lowering, ears flicking toward me. She had been waiting—for *this*. For my truth.

And at that moment, I understood.

Horses don't care what you *say*, they care what you *feel*. They need congruence. When I hid my frustration, she pulled away. When I *owned it,* she came back.

That day, I learned one of the most important lessons of my life: I had spent so long holding in my anger, my sadness, my struggle. But burying emotions doesn't make them disappear. It only keeps me stuck.

The horse showed me a different way.

And I knew, if I wanted to move forward, truly move forward, I had to learn to be fully present. To breathe. To be in my body. To let go.

This was more than training to help others.

This was real healing for me.

Spokes of Insight

Reflection Prompt:
- Find a quiet place as you settle into this reflection.
- Give yourself permission to listen deeply to a quiet voice within.
- Where are you not expressing or being authentic with yourself?
- If you give that quiet part a voice to speak and be heard, what do you hear?

_____

_____

_____

_____

Breath and Body Activity:
- Find a quiet space and sit comfortably in a chair with a sturdy back.
- Invite your breath to move to the back of your body and feel the support of the chair behind you.
- Take a few breaths, allowing your exhale to be longer than the inhale. Breathe with intention and allow yourself to breath fully.
- Return to normal breathing and notice any sensations or awareness in your body. Jot a few notes.

_____

_____

_____

_____

Learning While Doing

~

Learning to Ride

I came to Star Peak Stables expecting to learn about horses. I didn't realize how much they would teach me about *myself*.

The ranch was tucked into the mountainside, rugged and raw, the kind of place that demanded you rise to meet it. My wheelchair wasn't built for this terrain, only for the small concrete pad at the hitching post, which offered flat, hardpacked ground.

Fortunately, I wasn't there to roll. I was here to ride.

"Ready?" Julia asked, her sharp eyes assessing me once I was in the saddle.

"Sure," I said, masking the anxiety rising in my chest like dust in the afternoon sun. The first few rides revealed the truth: I didn't know much about riding. I had spent time with horses before, but never like this, never with such intentionality. And certainly, never with other riders watching. I felt small, out of place, an imposter among those who moved easily in this world.

But the horses didn't see me as small. They didn't care about my wheelchair, my crutches, or the way my legs didn't work like they'd used to. They met me exactly as I was, offering connection without expectation.

And that's when I began to *really* learn.

Riding wasn't just about control—it was about trust. If I sat too rigid, the horse stiffened beneath me. If my cues were too subtle, the horse ignored them. If I didn't lead, the horse simply stopped. I learned that leadership wasn't about force; it was about clarity. If I wanted the horse to move forward, I had to move forward, body, mind, and spirit.

I also learned that my greatest barrier wasn't my body. It was my mind.

On days when doubt crept in, when I felt like I didn't belong, the horse reflected it back on me and walked away. When I held tension, they resisted. But when I softened— when I breathed, let go, and *trusted*—the horse softened.

"Relax your jaw," Julia would remind me. "Drop your shoulders. Breathe."

Breath. Such a simple, involuntary function, yet a profound tool for transformation. Horses *know* when you're holding your breath. They feel your hesitation. They sense what you try to hide.

I stopped hiding.

If I was scared, I let myself be scared. If I was tired, I allowed myself to be tired. And as I learned to accept my own emotions, the horses met me there—with steadiness, with grace.

Over time, my confidence grew. The rhythmic movement of a trotting horse sent pulses of energy through my legs and spine, waking up muscles long unused. Each ride reconnected me—to the earth, to my own body, to the part of me that had never been broken.

The horses didn't heal me.

They *revealed* me.

And every time I slid off the saddle, I placed my hand on my horse's side, feeling the warmth of their body, the steady rise and fall of breath.

"Thank you for helping me."

Spokes of Insight

Reflection Prompt:
- What is something you want to learn, perhaps by going deeper into something you already know or do, or maybe by doing something totally new?
- Take some time to reflect on what it takes to trust yourself to move forward. Write a note to yourself about trust.

_____
_____
_____
_____
_____

Keep Learning Exercise:
- Gather some blank paper, old magazines, stickers and coloring pens.
- Create a visual representation of what you would like to keep learning.
- What is the next small step you will take toward that one new thing you want to learn?

Learning and Growing Never End

~

Keep Riding, Keep Learning

"Let's do the high trail ride today," Julia said as we prepared the horses for another lesson. At this point I'd been riding and learning from Julia and her horses for over a decade. Riding horses has become a huge part of my life.

I had been working on the low trail ride many times over the course of the summer.

Now, apparently, it was time to graduate upwards. I wasn't sure I was ready.

"Sure, let's do it," I said, pushing past a trickle of anxiety. I would be riding Badir, a sturdy mare whom I had ridden for many years now. We had done well together as a team, and I trusted her.

I knew the lower part of the ride well: out of the property to the dirt road, then through a kind of enchanted forest (as Julia called it), a short piece of softened path winding through a dense patch of pines, with a carpet of dry needles and soft moss sliced by beams of sunlight. Then up the rocky path to the back of the pasture.

The new path led us through more forested areas. When we reached the pasture, we headed left and started up the mountainous terrain, which took us through tall green pines and shimmering aspens. The horses followed the familiar (to them) path upward, stepping carefully over fallen tree limbs and branches. Eventually we rode up above the tree line, over the ten-thousand-foot mark of elevation. The forest gave way to open sky and rock, and we soon came to a small pond created by melting winter snow. Walking slowly into the cold, shallow water, Badir felt comfortable and familiar beneath me, but I still held my breath as we made our way into the middle of the pond. Swirling in my head were thoughts of everything that could go wrong.

What if she gets nervous and bucks me off? What if she slips on the rocks? What if, what it, what if?

And so, it went on and on and on.

Badir knew this pond and the surrounding area well. Nothing happened. Well, that's not true.

What happened was that I relaxed. I felt the familiar sensation of being high up in the mountains. Memories flowed from the times I had walked through forests and hills and mountains like these as a mountaineering instructor. I didn't realize how much I had missed the mountain air and the scent of the surrounding trees.

What *happened* is that as I sat atop Badir, embraced by the natural world in the melt pond, feeling so confident and comfortable, *I came back to myself.*

Many years of rides in the arena, diligent practice, growing competence and confidence, led to increasing challenges and increasing skills: walking and trotting the horse over poles on the ground, turning the horse around in a circle in an eight-foot box, increasing our gait from walking to trotting . . . and then finally riding over backcountry trails through high alpine meadows.

All this learning took place with horses named "Slick," "Symphony," "Peaches," "Pi," "Scooter," "Fairplay," "Star," "Badir" and "Salsa—-all of whom helped me find my balance and graciously forgave my ineptitudes. They helped me claim a newfound steadiness on their backs, while at the same time I reclaimed my inner strength. All that time, all that practice, bit by bit, hour by hour, horse by horse-an investment of time and money in myself that proved to be of immeasurable value.

Because the horses helped me find myself again.

Spokes of Insight

Reflection Prompts:
- I share in this chapter a deep trust built over the years with the many horses in my life. I learned to trust myself too and that helped me move forward. The journey from arena riding to high alpine trails was built on consistent effort, patience, and small steps forward.
- Where in your life are you investing in slow, steady progress? How do you remind yourself that each small step matters?
- Reflect on a relationship in your life—human or animal—that has helped you grow in confidence and resilience. How did that trust develop over time?

_____
_____
_____
_____
_____

High Trail Moment Exercise:
- Find a quiet place in nature, or if that's not possible, close your eyes and visualize an open, expansive landscape.
- Imagine yourself—moving from a place of comfort into the unknown. What does your "high trail" look like?
- What support (inner or outer) do you need to move forward?
- When you're ready, take a physical step—whether it's a small action toward a goal or a literal walk outside—to embody your courage and commitment.
- And remember to celebrate!

_____
_____
_____
_____
_____

Closing the Circle

Transformation & Healing

~

Windchime

Eight years had passed since the accident, yet I was still holding on—both literally and figuratively.

The mangled remains of my bicycle were stored in my garage, a twisted frame of metal and wire, gathering dust like an artifact from another life. I couldn't bring myself to throw it away. It was more than wreckage, it was *proof.* Proof that I had once been strong, fast, upright. That I had *moved* through the world on my own terms. That I had lived a life unbound by wheels of any kind.

Letting go of that bike felt like letting go of *her*—the version of myself before everything changed. And I wasn't ready.

Then one day, I mentioned the bike to a friend who was also an occupational therapist. Without hesitation, she said, "Let's turn it into something new."

I stared at her. "Like what?"

"A windchime," she said, her eyes bright with possibility. "Something beautiful. Something that moves this hunk of metal forward."

Her words hit me in a place I wasn't expecting. For years, I had been stuck between two worlds—the past I longed to return to and the reality I didn't quite accept. Maybe, just maybe, I was ready for something different.

"Okay," I said. "Let's do it."

That Thursday evening, we set up a shop on my back porch. My friend brought the tools needed; a saw, a blowtorch, wire cutters. I brought my bike, still bearing the police evidence tag from the crash, as if it were a relic from some unsolved mystery.

She fired up the saw. Sparks flew.

I flinched. I hadn't expected it to feel *this* hard, watching the frame being cut into pieces. My stomach twisted as the saw bit through the metal, breaking apart something that had once carried me across miles of open road.

This was more than an art project. This was *surgery*.

I busied myself untangling brake cables, removing chain rings, trying to keep my hands moving so my mind wouldn't spiral. I was excited, terrified, grieving, hopeful—all at once.

For years, I had relied on structure. I liked plans and clear directions. But this? There was no blueprint. No guide. We were making it up as we went, trusting the process, piece by piece.

By nightfall, the chime had taken shape. The bottom bracket of the bike became the suspension platform. Brake cables strung together the sawed-off tubes, now repurposed into chime rods. The chain rings hung in a cascading pattern. And at the very bottom, the bike's rear reflector—once used to catch headlights on the road—was now a windcatcher, ready to dance in the breeze.

We hung the chime on a hook outside. For a moment, there was silence.

Then—*music*.

A soft, metallic melody as the night air set it in motion. The sound of something broken becoming *whole* again.

I exhaled.

This was it.

Letting go. Stepping forward. The proof that transformation is possible—not just for old bicycles, but for me.

A windchime, catching the wind. Making new music in the world.

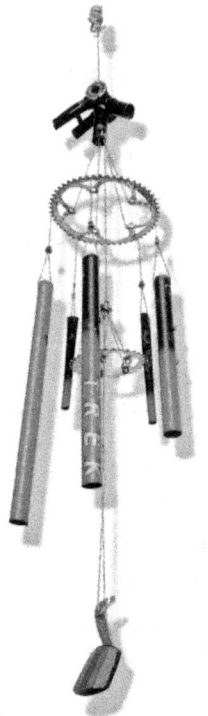

Terry's bicycle transformed into a windchime.

Spokes of Insight

Reflection Prompt:
- Think about a time when you had to break away from something to move forward. What was the experience like? How did it feel to you? Painful or freeing or both?
- Ask yourself if there is anything in your life that you've been holding on to for way too long. For example, maybe an object, a belief, or a memory?
- Write a few thoughts here.

_____
_____
_____
_____
_____

Transformation Creative Exercise:
- How might you imagine an object, a habit, or even a way of thinking that keeps you tethered to the past? What might it mean to release or transform it?
- If it's a physical object, could it be repurposed into art, like the bicycle into windchime? If it's a belief or a habit, how could you shift it into something more freeing?
- How would you transform it into something new? Do you notice resistance, relief, or both?
- After taking a small but symbolic step, journal about how you feel as you let go and create something new?

_____
_____
_____
_____
_____

Embrace the Journey- Not the Destination

~

A Wholehearted Life: It's Not About Walking

FOR MOST OF MY LIFE, I THOUGHT MOVEMENT—walking, running, biking—was the thing that gave my life meaning. But when the accident took that away, I woke up to something much bigger.

I could have stayed asleep. I could have resigned myself to a half-life of loss and limitation. But instead, I grabbed onto the threads of my life and refused to let go. And what I discovered is that this journey was never about walking. It was about *where* I chose to go.

Before the accident, I was floating—adrift in unfulfilling relationships, restless in my work, and stuck in a cycle of distraction, as if I was waiting for something to happen *to* me instead of realizing that I had the power to create my own life. The crash knocked the hesitation right out of me. It stripped me down to my rawest self, forcing me to confront the truth: I had been paralyzed *long before* I lost the ability to walk freely without braces, crutches or wheelchair.

The injury didn't just take something away. It gave me a chance to build a life with intention, to choose where I wanted to go instead of wandering aimlessly. It made me *pay attention*.

And so, I choose to move forward.

I chose to teach—fully and wholeheartedly.

Returning to my middle-school gymnasium, I couldn't just bark orders and throw out a ball anymore. I had to refine my skills. I had to become a better communicator, a sharper observer, and a more engaged leader. My wheelchair wasn't a barrier; it was simply how I moved. I would roll instead of stroll.

I chose adventure, not limitation.

The kayak became my vehicle to wild places. Handcycles took me across the vast landscapes of Colorado. Horses carried me to places my body could no longer reach on its own. I learned to trust, to lead, to be gentle and strong at the same time. Movement didn't stop; it just transformed.

I chose to face the darkness.

There were times when the weight of my grief, anger, and loss felt unbearable. I stood on the edge—of cliffs, of despair, of giving up. But instead of falling into the abyss, I turned inward. I let the light crack through the pain, allowing it to shape me rather than destroy me.

I chose love.

Sharon met me in my most vulnerable moments—when I was raw, exposed, uncertain. She stayed. She held on even when I tried to push her away. She helped me learn that I didn't have to go through life alone. That receiving love could be just as powerful as giving it.

Now, I invite you.

This wholehearted life—it's available to you, too.

You don't need a catastrophic event to wake you up. You can start now. Take a step—even a small one—toward what calls you. Move past your comfort zone, because that's where life begins. Ask for help. Pay attention to the whispers of your own heart.

And, most importantly, *stay awake*. There is always more life to be lived.

Spokes of Insight

Reflection Prompt:
- Reflect on the growth you have experienced over the course of this guidebook.
- What areas of your life do you feel are more expansive and freer?
- What areas may still need more time and attention?

_____
_____
_____
_____

- In your own words, reflect and write about how your understanding of WholeHearted living has evolved.
- Write a note of gratitude and acknowledgement for your WholeHearted Journey.

_____
_____
_____
_____

Wheel of Life Closing Activity:
- Divide the circle below into segments. Like pizza!
  - Label each segment with the areas of your life from the prompt.
  - Reflect on how you are attending to each of those segments. Are any of these areas out of balance?
- Now revisit your first Wheel of Life.
  - Consider how the areas have shifted in balance and what needs your attention.
- What next step will you take to bring that slice into balance?
- Place it somewhere visible as a reminder of your journey.
- Celebrate your WholeHearted Journey!!

Notes for My WholeHearted Journey   Date:_____

Notes for My WholeHearted Journey   Date:_____

Notes for My WholeHearted Journey   Date:_____

Notes for My WholeHearted Journey   Date:_____

Notes for My WholeHearted Journey   Date:_____

Notes for My WholeHearted Journey   Date:_____

Notes for My WholeHearted Journey   Date:_____

Notes for My WholeHearted Journey   Date:_____

Notes for My WholeHearted Journey   Date:_____

Notes for My WholeHearted Journey   Date:_____

About the Author

TERRY CHASE HAS ALWAYS BEEN DRAWN TO ADVENTURE. Growing up exploring the wooded trails of Long Island, New York, and later discovering the vast beauty of the Colorado mountains and desert plains, she developed a deep love for the outdoors—a passion that still fuels her today.

A natural teacher, Terry, has a knack for breaking down ideas into practical, easy-to-understand concepts, always weaving in a sense of fun and discovery. She brings a unique perspective to her work, shaped by over three decades of living—and thriving—with a spinal cord injury. Rather than slowing her down, this experience has sharpened her ability to help others create bold visions for the future and take tangible steps toward making them reality.

With an impressive array of degrees and certifications—including a Nursing Doctorate (ND), earned after her injury, Terry is a lifelong learner who believes in the power of resilience, curiosity, and action. She lives life full-out, embracing every opportunity to kayak, cross-country ski, hand-cycle, and, whenever possible, partner with horses.

Terry calls Western Colorado home, where she shares life's adventures with her partner, Sharon, their two energetic dogs, and one very wise, old cat.

Work with Dr. Terry Chase

Dr. Terry Chase is a powerhouse speaker, author, and coach who brings a wealth of experience in healthcare, education, leadership, and professional development. With advanced degrees and decades of hands-on expertise, she delivers inspiring keynotes, immersive workshops, and transformative coaching that leave a lasting impact.

A master facilitator, Dr. Chase blends experiential learning with real-world insights, guiding corporate teams, healthcare professionals, and educators toward breakthrough moments in leadership, communication, and team dynamics. Her engaging presentations and interactive sessions help organizations cultivate resilience, foster collaboration, and drive meaningful change.

For those seeking deeper growth, Dr. Chase offers individual and team coaching to unlock potential and navigate professional and personal transitions with clarity and confidence. Her signature *A WholeHearted Life* message empowers clients to lead and live with purpose, courage, and ease.

For more about working with Dr. Terry Chase see: https://drterrychase.com/

Other Books by the Author

www.ingramcontent.com/pod-product-compliance
Lightning Source LLC
Chambersburg PA
CBHW081156070526
44583CB00021B/2863